THE

EMOSEWA

WOMAN !

SECOND EDITION
SECOND PRINTING, MAY 2013

Safe Haven Publishing Company

SAFE HAVEN PUBLISHING COMPANY
P.O. Box 4673
Beaufort, SC 29903

ISBN: 978-0615824178

First Edition: ISBN #978-0-557-26333-2

_____CONTENTS_____

Plus the Special Holiday Piece.......

MAN WITH THE GOLDEN WINGS
103

EMOSEWA

My Regal Queen

I bow down to Your Beauty

Your Eternal Inner Light of Love

You are, Emosewa

My Instant Inspiration

My Sweet Aroma of Sensual Serenity

You are, Emosewa

I know--There's never enough words to describe

You Wonderful Women!

But, the poem below is my monumental attempt to.

Compliments Of Quality...Quite A Few

TRIBUTE

My Special Lady, didn't You know, YOU are a Sweet, Beautiful,
Comforting, Wonderful, Fabulous, Fantastic, Amazing, Great,
Glamorous, Gleaming, Alluring, Sincere, Sexy, Wild, Warm, Exotic,
Erotic, Voluptuous, Soothing, Sensuous, Hypnotic Gorgeous
Woman?

A Celestial Butterfly,

Hot-Chocolatey,

Cocoa Buttery,

Brown-Sugary,

Highly-Intelligent,

Heavenly-Bodily,

Dark & Lovely,

Elegantly-Proportioned,

Silky Smooth,

Luscious,   Breathtaking,   Passionate,   Vibrant,

Virtuous,   Vivacious,   Intense,

Energetic,   Exquisite,   Seductive,

Sensational,   Sensitive,   Serene,

Soft,   Sophisticated,   Soulful,   Steamy,

Sticky-Sweet,   Subtle,   Succulent,

Sultry,   Super-Fine,   Supple,

Embracing,   Enchanting,   Enhancing,

Enjoyable,   Enriching,   Enticing,

Excellent,   Exciting,   Extraordinary,

Sizzling,   Sparkling,

SPIRITUALLY-ENLIGHTENED,

Charismatic,   Mesmerizing,   Intoxicating,

Stylish,   Stunning,   Strong,

Determined,   Powerful,   Loyal,

Serious,   Light-Hearted,   Jazzy,

Dazzling,   Tantalizing,   Temptuous,

Truthful,   Faithful,   Flexible,   Real,

Outspoken,   Cool,   Independent,

Innovative,   Inspiring,   Intuitive,

Assertive,   Attractive,   Diverse,

Decisive,   Deliberate,   Dependable,

Direct To The Point,

Persistent,   Proud,   Responsible,

Enthusiastic!

*** My   Regal   Ebony   Queen***

YOU   Are

Embellishing,

Honey-comb Delicious,

Spicy Cinnamon-Tasty,

Ebony-Cream,

Absorbing,

Adoring,

Affectionate,

Ageless,

Appealing,

Arousing,

Awesome,

A COMPLEX WOMAN,

YOU Are Always

Radiant, Ravishing, Refreshing,

Phenomenal, Captivating, Profound,

Protective, Provocative, Provoking, Potent,

Striking, Flawless, Healthy, Gentle, Loving,

Kind, Unique, Natural, Delicate, Deserving,

Infinitely-Beautiful,

Nurturing, Unbelievable, Talented, Colorful,

Nourishing, Incredible, Intimate,

The Twilight Irresistible Eternal ANGEL of my Heart.

YOU Are My Romantic Ultimate

Beautiful   Black   Woman,

YOU Are Quality

YOU Are ROYALTY!

I AM

THE EMOSEWA WOMAN

I Am The Emosewa Woman

I Am Powerful

I Am The Fortress Of Life

My Intensity

Quenches The Fire Of Your Desire For Me

Into Spiritual Reverence

Of My Inner Beauty

Not My Physicality

I Am The Emosewa Woman

I Am Authority

I Am That Woman Of GOD

My Sovereignty

Reigns Supreme Over Your Infatuation Of Me

Influencing Your Respect

Of My Personal Space

Not My Flesh

I Am Emosewa

I Am Awesome

I Am.... The Emosewa Woman!

SERENITY   SPEAKS

Serenity speaks

When I'm with You

I hear sweet Peace of Mind

total bliss

when we kiss

I hear silent soul songs

complete calm

while drawing finger circles

inside your palm

I hear "I Love only You"

Deep Inside

where we do

our rhythmic Love ride

I hear Tranquility

flowing

through our Life

knowing

when Serenity speaks

I'm with You

When Serenity speaks

I hear

You

DEEP

Deep,

Into

The

Empty

Warmth

Sliding in

Squeezing in

Suddenly gripped

by

Moans

From the abyss of pleasure

The depths of lust

Screaming and singing loudly

Dancing

Deeply,

to

The music of Love.

SMOOTH MAHOGANY

or

"What Our Eyes See—Isn't"

Smooth   Mahogany

Chestnut   Skin

Hazel   Eyes

Summer   Sin

Buttery   Beige

Auburn   Hair

Copper   Lips

Fatal   Lair

Mocha   Brown

Coffee   Thigh

Bronze   Nails

Deadly   Pie

Smooth   Mahogany

Chestnut   Skin

Smooth   Mahogany

Lost   Within

THE SUGAR ZONE

Welcome to The Sugar Zone

Where Sweetness Resides

She's never alone

She makes YOUR COFFEE Rise

She'll Lick your tongue

She'll Blow your mind

She'll have you sprung

She's just that Fine

She's Smooth and Tasty

Soft to the Touch

She's in your Love Pastry

Oh—She's too much!

She Lives in your Caramel Love

Swims in your Hot Chocolate

Of Her you'll never get enough

She's Definitely Succulent

Her Spice is Down South

Where She meows the Soul

She Melts in your mouth

Right out of that Brown-Sugar Bowl

So,…You can only lick your lips when She Arrives

Welcome to The Sugar Zone, where Sweetness Resides

****

The Day I saw Her, I had to ask

"Sweet Sugar Candy Girl, how do I

Savor Your Flavor?"

And with a coy smile, She Whispered

"You know how Baby,

Down Here in The Sugar Zone."

JUST FRIENDS—NO MORE

Can't be   We

Can't be   Us

Can't be   Love…

How Could It Be?

We're just Friends.

APPLE

She's so supple

So sweet to eat

My hands itch with desire

To touch Her

To feel Her flexibility

Flowing in my mouth,

Pliable,

As I taste Her buoyancy of Love—

Her ephemeral core of ecstasy

Amenable and yielding

Only…

To me

THE EYES OF LYNDA

The Looking Eyes of Lynda

Reveal

Truth Beyond Beauty Limitless

Love Beyond Life Abundant

Peace Beyond Silence Serene

They Reveal Desire Divine

The Laughing Eyes Of Lynda

Speak

Wisdom Beyond Words Flowing

Music Beyond Angels Singing

Ecstasy Beyond Lips Kissing

They Speak Deep Inside

The Luminating Eyes Of Lynda

Blossom

Attraction Beyond Hearts Beating

Feelings Beyond Smiles Blushing

Sighs Beyond Bodies Merging

They Blossom Love Alive

The Eyes Of Lynda Blossom Her

PRINCESS LIGHT

Who is Princess Light?
She is the light of dawn
Waking up Life with a coy smile
and Eyes
that twinkle in the Night

Her Breath of Expression
Sings through souls
She lights up Life
So Shiny, Shining Bright
She is Princess Light

Full of Beauty, sunshine,
Happiness and Life

Her Rays   of Joy
Swims inside
Hearts filled with
Only
Love,
When She is around.

Who is She?
Who Is This Regal Princess
Dominating, Demanding so much Attention
Surrounding Her with such
Overwhelming Beauty
Brightness, Sunshine and
Happiness and Life

She is only the Light
Waking up Life
With a Coy Smile and
Eyes that Sparkle, Twinkle
In The Night

She Is Princess   Light

She IS You

Brightening our Love
With Joy
Sunshine and Happiness
So Full of Life
So Very Bright

Princess Light!!

AROMA

My Name is Aroma
and
Aroma's Sweet Scent
Pierces your Breath

When you see me...
My Serene Symmetry
Explodes before you

When you hear me...
My Sensuous Sound
Swims inside you

When you feel me...
My Seductive Smoothness
Arouses all of you

And

When you breathe me...
My Sweet Scent
Pierces through you

Pierces your Breath

My Name is Aroma
and

Aroma Surrounds you
With Fragrance

My Fragrance of Love

THE CRUMBLE WOMAN

Each And Every Morning, As She Rises, She Begins To Fall
Apart.
Chips Of Her Life, Flying And Floating Away.
But, In The Evening, She Pieces Herself Together For Another
Tenuous Start
Plastering And Molding Back Into Her Form.

She Is The Crumble Woman
Crumbling With Each Step
Crumbling Through Life
But,… She Is A Survivor

Throughout Her Dismal Day She Disintegrates—Yet Still She
Strives,
Even As Her Soul And Mind Fades Away.
And Late At Night, She Doesn't Sleep—It's Her Way Of
Knowing,
She's Alive.
It's Her Way Of Knowing, She'll Survive.

She Is The Crumble Woman
Crumbling With Each Step
Crumbling Through Life
Yet,… She Is A Survivor

Since The Dawn Of Her Life, Like Sand, She Has Shifted And
Sprinkled Everywhere,

Seeping Through Her Heart—The Pain Of Existence.
But As Dusk And God Approaches—She Realizes, He Does
Really
Care,
Giving Her Victory And Strength Over All Of Her...
Crumbling Life.

She Is The Crumble Woman
Crumbling With Every Step
Crumbling Through Life
And Yes,...
She Is The Survivor

****

She walks with a limp

because She's losing herself.

However, She's full of strength

She has,......GOD's help.

"PSST" !

Hey man you see that

Chocolate Sista over there?"

"Yeah Her."

"She wants to give you some of Her

Chocolate Ice Cream.

She wants to give it---

Bad and smooooth…"

"Do you want some?"

ENIGMA

"Call me what you like.
Ignore me as if I don't exist.
Label me as you have
and
always will. But, you'll never figure
me out."

"I call myself Enigma.
And you will never know me,
unless you ask—Properly.
Then,
I may tell you…That is, If,
I'm in the mood."

ONE-WAY LOVE

Have You Ever Been In Love?

And Not Have That Love Given Back?

Yes…

You Wanted Total Happiness

But, Only Got Lonely Restlessness

You Love With All Your Heart

Only To Have It Torn Apart

A One-Sided Image Of Just You…

Giving Your All

I Wish Love Wasn't So Painful

Where Being In Love…

Is Alone Inside You

A One-Sided Joy

A One-Way Love.

WOMAN

WOMAN, your beauty exudes from your body

And I can taste your essence,

As your mind caresses those around you.

Peaceful serenity you possess,

An inner calm that puts hearts to rest,

A trembling sensation flowing through the air

Wherever you may be.

WOMAN, you are the sun shining rays of love.

You are the breeze that soothes painful memories.

You are a stunning angel, fallen from the sky,

And lightning bows at your path

While thunder rolls at your command.

You are a Goddess, who offers the wine of

Happiness

And receives eyes of worship.

You are a sparkling waterfall seen from afar,

That lights up the top of the world.

Your beauty fulfills its needs and your

Mind does as it please.

WOMAN, you are gorgeous,

And beyond my words, mind, and soul,

I have never met anyone like you.

And I never will!

EUPHORIA

The next time you see Her

You will see a sense of Pride

The next time you see Her

You will see inside Her Beauty

Inside Her Happiness

You will see... Euphoria

The next time you touch Her

You will feel the Blissfulness of Her soul

The next time you touch Her

You will feel the softness of Her Kiss

In Her Lips

You will feel...Euphoria

The next time you hear Her

You will hear the drumbeat of Her Love

The next time you hear Her

You will hear Her singing Heart

Singing in your mind

You will hear...Euphoria

Euphoria--We need You...

The Next Time

To See

To Touch

To Hear

Your Greatness

Your Euphoric

Exotic

Ecstatic

Expression...

Of Love

COPPER GIRL

Oh My God!

Every Time

I See Her

My Eyes Expand

And...

POP!

That's My Copper Girl

She Has The Smoothest

Bronze Skin

Long Reddish-Brown Hair

WOW!

That's My Copper Girl

She's Sleek

Like Pure Mahogany

Statuesque As An Amazon

From--Mythology

Oh YEAH!

That's My Copper Girl

She Knows She's

Got It Going On

Here And Above

She Exudes

Absolutely Nothing But...

Deep Love

And YES!

I Adore Her

My Beautiful--

Copper Girl!

ANTHEM

PEOPLE…WE ARE!

BLACK…WE ARE!

GREAT…WE ARE

ALWAYS!

MIDNIGHT MISTRESS

She crawls in midnight seeking Her victims.

Your man is Her man.

She's always willing to spread Herself wide-open

to entice his Nature.

She's available to any wandering eye--full of lust.

And if your man wanders

She makes him Her slave

in the deep of night

while giving away Her midnight Secret

bubbling and boiling between Her

moist Forbidden Zone.

And as your man peeks inside, to seek out

the Secret,

He is suddenly sucked into Her seething Vacuum

and never returns.

~She's willing to appease~

She's willing to be...

the Mistress.

She's always willing..

to steal your man

in midnight.

CARAMEL FEEL-GOOD

She wants some Caramel Feel Good

some Hot Sticky Candy

throbbing inside Her mouth

She yearns for Sweet Brown Sugar

sprinkled on Her tongue

sliding down Her throat

She's thirsty for some Steamy Hot Chocolate

spilling off Her lips

dripping all over Her

breathing Bosom

She looovves...

Caramel Feel Good

She looovves...

Hot Sticky Candy--Inside

Her mouth

IRRESISTIBLE

When I hear

Your Serene Voice approach

I start to itch...

with desire

When I see

Your Voluptuous Beauty enter

I start to evaporate...

with lust

When I smell

Your Sweet Scent swirling

around me

I faint...

with love

And as

You awaken me with Your Tender Touch

I feel...

aroused

Then I taste

You,

with complete abandonment

You are...

Irresistible

SHE SITS ON A SHELF

On a shelf she sits,

Placed by Him

Right between the copper girl

With the chipped heart

And the older woman on the pedestal.

On a shelf she sits,

Waiting impatiently

For Him to love her.

She's not like the others,

She thinks.

He won't leave me here, unwanted.

Not like He left them.

So she waits for Him

To take her down

And rescue her.

On a shelf she sits,

Alone with the other

Forgotten trophies.

Now, she hopes to fall

And break

Into tiny pieces of escape.

Then she'll know for sure

She's free from the shelf

Free

From Him.

THE NO-GIRL

There's This Beautiful Girl I Know

She Always Seems to Say No

To The Most Irrelevant Of Things

It's Almost As If She Wants To Sing

A Negative Soprano

Instead A Violin--She Plays A Piano

Of Tears, Softly Refusing Advances Made,

Screaming No, In The Shade

Leading Light Away From The Day

To A Darker Reality

Of Her,

Just Saying No...To Everything

CHEERLEADER

A Life in Celebration,
All smiles of Her secret joy
Of cheerleading Life.
She is a cheerleader of Life,
A Life in Celebration.
She's just Unique that way.

She's a cheerleader of Life
Brimming with Enthusiasm,
Celebrating always,
Smiling always,
Overflowing with Love.
She's just Unique that way.

Her Smiles are all,
Her Laughter large,
Her Spirit Great,
Her Eyes bright—glowing with a Secret,
Her Secret.
She's just Unique that way.
A Life in Celebration.
She's just Unique that way,

What else can I say

SIMPLY LISA

The Moment

I saw You stride through the door

I felt Your Strength

Instantly

Your Essence

Your Regal Beauty

Your Presence

Your Aura,

Spiritually

You are...

Simply Lisa

THREE INVITATIONS

1ST INVITATION
(SURRENDER)

PLEASE…

DON'T

SLIP

INTO

ME

JUST FALL

2ND INVITATION
(SERENITY)

PLEASE…

DON'T

SLIP

INTO

ME

JUST

FALL

AND

JOIN ME

3RD INVITATION
(SALVATION)

PLEASE…

DON'T

SLIP

INTO

ME

AND

SLIP

OUT

JUST FALL

AND

JOIN ME

BECOME…

A PART

OF ME

ASPIRIN

"Not tonight
I have a headache."
Now,

Why do You say that?--

Because You can.

But…

I

Have the right Relief

That soothing Medication

Sliding in Your Sugar Zone

Massaging Your Temple of Love

Relieving You to say...

"YES!--TONIGHT!"

BLACK BUTTERFLY

(Dedicated to RM Green)

Slender Wings
Fluttering Beauty and Allure

An Ebony Radiance of Flight,
Through Souls of Despair.

A Dark Beauty
Bringing Hope and Salvation,
Gliding through the air of Disbelief.

She is…
A Beautiful Butterfly of Faith.

A Black Butterfly of Love,
Floating through our Thoughts.

She is…
A Silent LoveSong,
Hovering in Hearts,
Waiting to be heard by All.

Her Slender Wings
Fluttering Beauty and Allure.

She is Ebony—A Dark Beauty.

She is…Strength.

She is…The Black Butterfly.

MISS FABULOUS

Didn't I see You the other day

The other day on television

Looking Great
Looking Fine
Looking Fabulous

Wasn't that You?

Miss Fabulous

Wasn't that You singing this morning

Singing that song of Love

Sounding Smooth
Sounding Sensual
Sounding Fabulous

Was that You?

Miss Fabulous

Aren't You appearing at the ball this week

The society ball of Beauty

Wearing Your Elegance
Wearing Your Pride
Wearing Your Fabulous Smile

Aren't You...

Miss Fabulous?

Yes You are!

I see You everyday—in my mind's eye

Being Fabulous,

Looking Fabulous,

Inside and out.

You are…Miss Fabulous!

SIREN

She was who She was

Ancient

Alluring

Seductive

Her Chocolate Lips

Her Swaying Hips

Her Ebony Eyes

Mesmerized

Men and Women alike

Stealing their hearts

Swallowing their souls

Transforming their Love

into

Hers

of

Deceit and Admiration

~Her Siren Seduction~

RETRIBUTION

You See Her Everyday
Act A Certain Way
You Wonder Why She Does
It's Only Just Because
She's Black Like That
Because...

Black Is Back

Did You Really Forget?
Wisdom Is Not Sick
I Thought You Knew That
It's Just The Way She Acts
She's Black Like That
Because...

Black Is Back

Just Remember This
As She Raises Her Fist
She's Here To Stay
In Her Certain Way
She's Black Like That
And Just Because...

Black Is Back!

CARAMEL NO MORE?

Has Your Caramel faded, withered and disappeared?

Have You lost Your Brilliance of Color

Your Caramel Cream of Love

Or

Are You just an Amorphous Memory

Of Caramel Lost...Your connection to Us?

Have You changed?

Are You...

Caramel no more?

ON THIS DAY (November 4, 2008)

On This Day
I stumbled upon Her Ebony form in the early mist of
dawn
Years of darkness surrounded Her
A strange statue of Great Beauty
Shrouded in secrecy
A complete mystery

However, On This Day, She was facing the sunrise,
For the first time in eons.
On This Day
Change, Hope and Truth will hold hands
To allow this Ancient Shrine to shine through.
On This Day
This Ancient statue will awaken
And become...Alive

I fell back in awe
Fear slipping through me
Motionless I was
As She slowly turned toward me
Then Her Eyes lit up
And with a smile,
On This Day,
She whispered...
Finally!!

A NUBIAN KISS

In the deep dark
I thought they were Her lips
Waking me up
But who I saw
Was not She (Syawla)
Breathing in my face.
The eyes I didn't recognize
Yet,...so close to mine
And when she floated
Back a step,
She was new,
A soft shadow,
A Nubian Seraph
Not Who I Thought She
Would be
Not my personal Wraith
Just a new muse
Leaving Her
Angelic Lyrical Rhythm
Imprinted upon my soul.
A Nubian Seraph
Loving me...with Wisdom

THE WISDOM KEEPERS
(Dedicated to the Memory of DEBRA D. GRIFFIN)

We see Them everywhere--The Wisdom keepers

The Matriarchs of our lives

Guardians of Truth

Sisters to Love

Enforcers of Discipline.

The Ones Who raised us and kept us safe.

The Ones who said GOD is Always

And Love is GOD.

Our Idea of Strength when we were weak.

The Protectors of our self-respect, Who said,

"Let no one put You down, You are much more
than that."

We see Them everywhere

The Discoverers of the lost

Teachers of Faith

Friends to Insight

Keepers of Wisdom.

The Wisdom Keepers--Who are They?

Your Mother and Mine.

A-DREAM-FOR-A-DAY

She-was-having-a-Wonderful-Dream

She-Dreamed-She-was-a-Queen

She-Dreamed-She-was-sitting-on-Her-throne

The-Thunder-of-applause-filling-the-palace

And-as-everyone-began-to-open-their-mouths-to-say

She-suddenly-woke-up-to-the-sweetest-sound-of

"Happy-Mother's-Day!!"

ABSENTIA

My name is ABSENTIA
but, I'm not absent.
However, no one seems
to see or hear me.
But I'm everywhere.
But, to you all
I'm nowhere.
A nothing woman
satisfying your perverted dreams.
When you need me,
then you see me.
But only with your polluted vision of
My Eternal Black Beauty,
exploited for your lustful
gain of pleasure,
your manipulative pursuit of
My Greatness,
which you are afraid of.
My name is ABESENTIA
but, I'm not absent.
You will see Me,
but, properly.
And you will definitely hear me
Roar.
My name is ABSENTIA
and
I am not!...

Absent.

HUMBLED BY BEAUTY AS YOU DO
WHAT YOU DO

Every time I See You!--I am Humbled by Your Beauty

There You Are...
And Suddenly I Have Googly Eyes

In A Flash, My Mouth Is Wide Open--It Won't Shut.

And That's Each And Every Time I See You!

You...How Do You Do What You Do--To Me?

This Feeling Of Awe Inside Me

Overwhelms Me

By You Just Being Near Me

Smothers Me

By You Just Blessing Me--With Your Presence.

You...How Do You Do What You Do--To Me?

This Feeling Of Weakness

Wobbles Through Me

Engulfs Me

When I Try To Say...

"Hello, How Are You?"

I Fumble As Only A Timid "Hi" Is Uttered

And I Lower My Eyes

Before Your Beauty Consumes Me

Again.

You...Why Do You Do What You Do--To Me?

Because...YOU Can

I Am Humbled By Your Beauty

ALWAYS

SHE always visits me in the very
deep of night.

And SHE always rises out of eternity
from the foot
of my bed.

And like a wraith, SHE slides silently
in
besides me.

Then SHE whispers in my ear,
Thoughts of Love.

SHE kisses me, with Words of Wisdom.

SHE caresses me, with Poetry.

SHE tells me SHE Loves me
and will always come back,
again and again.

And even though I'm afraid to sleep at night,
I always expect HER.

SHE is...
my Inspiration
SHE is...
where Words come from.

Always.

SYAWLA

I call Her Syawla

and She visits me

every night in my dreams

She surrounds me

with Her Breath of Inspiration

while clutching my soul

with Lustful Passion of Words

Moaning Verses of Love

humming ecstasy with Her Fingers

then She bites me with a Poem

I call Her Syawla

and She visits me

every night in my dreams...

Leaving Her Kiss Inside me

Note: This poem is a variation of my poem "Always", which is Syawla spelled backwards.

BONDED

When You are in love

My words kiss You

When You are in joy

My words laugh with You

When You are in misery

My words weep for You

When You are in pain

My words bleed for You

My words are You...

Always

BREATH-BEAT OF YOU

You...
A-Breathing-Wisp,
A-Breathing-Breeze...
Of-Serenity
A-Soothing-Gasp
Heaving-In-My-Ear
Unbalancing-My-Spirit--

I-Feel-Your-Breath,
Your-Beat-As-You-Speak
Your
Voice
Sounding
Like-Whispers
Of-Exhaling-Love

That

Always-Makes-Me-Feel-Like-Fainting
Always-Makes-Me-Feel-like...
Floating-Away.

Your-Soft-Voice
Your-Siren-Words
Breathing-Inside-My-Head
Breathing-Inside-My-Heart
Aspiring-Inside-Me...
Totally.

You...
I-Feel-Your-Breath
The-Breath-Of-You
A-Breathing-Wisp,
A-Breathing-Breeze...
Of-Ecstasy

DISCLOSURE

Wonderful Woman

Are You married?

Do You have a boyfriend?

Because if You do,

We can be as close as

You want me to be

But,

Without the Intimacy

You see,

I must take Responsibility

By treating You

With the upmost Respect

And not defect

To Lust

You

Are more than that

REMEMBER

There's always the light of dawn

And just like You,

There's always a You in You

A Genesis of Life blossoming eternally

Within You

There's always a You in You

Silently whispering in Your Soul,

Echoing Your Thoughts throughout

the night,

Blessing You with Wisdom

Of a Delicate Life

And like the light of dawn

Will always return

Remember...

There's always a You in You

JUST FOR ME

I think of You

How come You don't think of Me

How come You don't see

the inner Me

trying to be

what I want You to see

How come You won't be--my personal Lady

How come You won't be--just for Me

UNCONDITIONALLY

You First

Me Last

I Listen

You Talk

I Don't Want A Car

But I'll Buy You One

Am I Crazy?--No, Just In Love

Unconditionally

And Not With Myself

But With You

As I Said...

You First

Me Last

A SALACIOUS LOOK (FOR JUST...ONLY ME)

A Salacious Look
She Has It
The Way Her Eyes Twist And Spin
Or So I Think--At Just Only Me
The Way She Talks And Walks
With Her Hips
Swaying
The Way She Licks And Puckers
Her Lips
Pointing
Or So I Think--At Just Only Me

The Way She Says "Oops...!"
As She Drops...Anything
Then Bends Over To Pick It Up
Or So I Think--For Just Only Me
The Way Her Warm Breathing
Breezes By Me
As She Sits Next To Me
Arousing Me
Or So I Think--For Just Only Me

The Way
Her Essence
Her Sensuality
Her Lust
Her Intense Appetite
Gyrating
Or So I Think--Toward Me
Has Me...
Seeing Her Amiable Pleasant
Voluptuous Ways
Salaciously
Or So I Think--For Just Only Me

The Salacious Look...
She Has It

She's Definitely Got It!
For Just...Only Me
Or So I Think...

LEGACY LOST

··

As I entered the Palace

I drew out my Ebony Sword

But the Throne of my Love

Was empty

"Where are You, my Queen!"

I shouted

"Over here", She replied

I turned around

But I could not see Her

"Over here", She whispered

I walked toward the sound of Her voice

And there She stood

As I looked right through Her

With outstretch arms she said

"I'm fading away my Love"

"The thoughts of our People, of Me, They no longer

think of"

I frantically reached for Her

As she started to disappear

On Her face, a sad smile and a single tear

"Don't forget me my Love"

And then She was gone

"I won't...my Queen"

"I won't...my Love"

PROPOSAL

My eyes lick in Your Beauty

My ears taste Your Soul

You are the Greatest Truth

My Eternal Love of the day

You are the Future in my life

And I would be honored

If You would be my Wife

I Love Only. . .

The You in You

SOMETIMES I'LL WAKE UP IN THE MIDDLE OF THE NIGHT AND SEE WORDS CLEAR AS DAY IN MY MIND. I USUALLY DISMISSED THEM FROM MY MIND, BUT THIS POEM I DECIDED TO WRITE DOWN. IT'S FUNNY--THE TITLE, THE WORDS WERE ALL THERE AS IF I WROTE THEM IN A DREAM.

MERGE

I want to put me

into you

Sliding all

through you

Solving that Mystery

of us

Doing together

as one

Being as One

Being. . .Love

SYLKIE'S SOLILOQUY
So...

She Speaks,
Sensual
Sentiments
Separating Sagacity,
Satisfying
Sacred
Soft
Secretive
Seductive
Serene Sounds.

So...

She Sings,
Sweetly
Shrewd
Sincere
Sexual Silence,
Sharing
Shrouded
Soulful
Spellbinding Sensations.

So...

She's Solely Sylkie,
She's Sylkie Solely
Saying
Softspoken
Smooth
Syllables
Symbolizing
Silky (Sylkie)
Symmetry.

She's Solely Sylkie

She's Sylkie...

Solely

HEAT OF THE MOMENT

Her thoughts are dripping

listless love from between

Her inner warmth

of emotional rapture.

Her words are dripping

wet whispers from inside

Her heaving breath

of heated despair.

Her eyes are dripping

true tears from behind

Her glaring gothic gaze

of

"I must have you."

She is...

in the heat of the moment.

She is...

dripping with Love.

FOREPLAY

You know what

I would Looovve to take my tongue

and lick You between

Your   Thoughts

Taste Your Mind for Inspiration

Before Exploding You with Words

A VISION OF AWE

When She stepped onto the bus,
I didn't noticed Her.
When I did...
Silence became Silent.
The sudden screaming of Her Beauty
Blinded me with a flash of light
As the Sight of Her became nothing but
A Silhouette of a Shadow
As She sat down by me!
My Vision of Her~An Aftermath~
A Vision of Awe
An Emosewa Woman.

With my eyes and mouth agape,
The sound of lust shrieking in my mind,
Speechlessness struck me in my chest.
My heart thumping so loud,
I just knew She heard it.
My ears drumming a beat of uneasiness
Only
I
Felt.
I was in total Awe as Her Perfume
Tickled me with arousement.
Then...
She looked at me and Smiled!
My soul fainted.
But, I didn't let Her know...
That I was melting inside
As I tried to smile back.
I was Awestruck with Her Aura.
Her Awesome Essence Emanating
In front of me,
A Vision of Awe
Truly again--An Emosewa Woman
To me.

Then, before I knew it--it was Her stop.
She got up, still Smiling,
Her Elbow brushing my shoulder,
As She rose like an Angel taking flight.
My shoulder, enjoying that Stimulating,
Smooth Sensual Brush, Slowly Spreading
Throughout my body and soul
As I watched Her slip away.
The sound of my heart still pounding--loudly.
Only I could hear what I saw...
A Vision of Awe
An Emosewa Woman.

NIKKI

She is the Mirror of my Soul

The Reflection of my Mind

She's the Eternal Woman

of my Poems

The One for...endless time

She is...Nikki

MAN

WITH THE

GOLDEN

WINGS!

It is Christmas Eve
and the snow is falling

on a lonely little house

in the countryside.

Come..., let us go inside and listen.

In this house, a little girl lies asleep

in her bed.

But sleep she doesn't stay, for she's

awakened by a bright light instead.

The light comes through her bedroom

window with warming colors.

And when she looks out her window,

she sees a man with wings on his back.

Golden Wings at that.

"Mama! Mama! Come look, come see!"

The little girl runs out her room as she cries.

"I just saw a man with Golden Wings outside.

He's tall and handsome, with a great big smile.

And his arms are full of nice shiny things.

Mama, who do you think this man is with

Golden Wings?"

Slowly her mother looks up from her rocking chair.

She is still young with fair eyes, but now has grey

hair.

"Hush girl," She barely speaks in a soft whisper.

"Don't come runnin' in here tellin' me

boldface lies.

Your mama ain't feeling well, and there ain't

no man with Golden Wings outside.

I'se know you'se excited cause Christmas

is coming.

But, ain't no lying gonna make dawn come

a runnin'."

"But, but mama, I ain't lyin! I did see this man

outside.

He, he, had a halo on his head too, to go with

his big smile.

His Wings moved slowly to keep the snow

off them,

and he wanted to say something to me.

But, I ran in here so I could get you to see

this man with Golden Wings."

"Honey,...listen, your eyes can play tricks on you.

And the snow can make you see things too.

I remember when I was excited for Christmas

at your age.

I saw a giant lion with a great big white beard.

Hmp, it was nothing but a dream, but, I sure

was scared."

The little girl hangs her head and quietly says

"Mama, I'm sorry."

"Baby, that's all right."

"But, listen child, I know we haven't

had much in our way of living.

And hardly anyone, nowadays, has been

in the Spirit for giving.

But you know I'se tried to make things right

for both of us, since your daddy died.

So, for your daddy, we both have to survive."

"Tell me more about daddy, what was he like?"

"Your daddy was a God-fearing man, who died

before you was born.

And he died seven years ago on Christmas morn.

He was on his way home with presents in his arms,

when he was lost in the snow.

And he never knew he would have a daughter,

He never knew he would be a father."

"Was he a nice man?"

"Of course he was."

"But enough of this, go on back to bed

and get some rest.

And when you get up, I'll have you a good

hot breakfast."

The little girl gives her mother a hug and whispers

"Merry Christmas Mama" and slowly

away.

"Merry Christmas to you too, sweetheart,"

her mother replies while watching her daughter's

silent stroll

as she suddenly feels the

emptiness of her own lonely soul.

Quietly she rises from her rocking chair,

walking to her own room with much pain to bear.

She climbs into bed, wiping away her tears,

and glancing out her window, she feels a slight

fear.

And when sleep descends on her eyelids, she

asks GOD, "Does anyone really care?"

******

******

******

"Mama! Mama! Wake-up, Wake-up!

He really was

here!"

The little girl's voice rings in her mother's ear.

"Come look, come look, come see for yourself,"

she says while pulling and dragging her mother out

of bed

to see what Christmas day had bred.

By the bedroom window laid many pretty gifts

nestled comfortably in a glittering snow drift.

Toys and clothes all neatly arrayed

placed carefully with Love and Harmony

by the Man with the Golden Wings.

But the most surprising gift of all

that the mother only saw...

was her husband's wedding ring.

She slowly bends down and picks it up

while her daughter asks

"Mama, was He an Angel?"

"Yes Dear," her Mother replies.

"And much more. He was your Daddy,

come home."

It is Christmas Day

and the snow has stopped falling.

And the lonely little house

in the countryside,

for today,

isn't so lonely.

ABOUT THE AUTHOR

Continuing with the same tradition and style as his first Book of Poetry (Love,Is,The Beautiful Black Woman)Vernon J. Davis Jr.'s Sophomore Book, "The Emosewa Woman!" is an ongoing Tribute of praise and admiration for the Awesome Women of the world. Hence, his title, "Emosewa", which is Awesome spelled backwards.

Mr. Davis's explicit sensitive style of poetry which is also spiritual and sensual in nature, comes from his 30+ years of observation, interaction, and bonding with the Wonderful Women he has met and still to meet--Using his words..."All Women are Emosewa!"

Read more about Vernon J. Davis Jr. at www.vernonjdavisjr.com

Also included in this Book--A Special Christmas Poem!

"We Write With Wondrous Words Welcoming Wisdom Willingly!"

Vernon J. Davis Jr.

www.ingramcontent.com/pod-product-compliance
Lightning Source LLC
Chambersburg PA
CBHW060323070426
42446CB00049B/2013